REALLY HORRIBLE HISTORY JOKES

KAREN KING AND PATIENCE COSTER

WINDMILL BOOKS
New York

Published in 2014 by Windmill Books, An Imprint of Rosen Publishing
29 East 21st Street, New York, NY 10010

First Edition

Editors: Patience Coster and Joe Harris
US Editor: Joshua Shadowens
All Images: Shutterstock
Layout Designer: Elaine Wilkinson
Cover Designers: Elaine Wilkinson and Trudi Webb

Library of Congress Cataloging-in-Publication Data

King, Karen, 1954 August 2–
Really horrible history jokes / by Karen King and Patience Coster.
    pages cm. — (Really horrible jokes)
Includes index.
ISBN 978-1-4777-9082-3 — ISBN 978-1-4777-9083-0 —
ISBN 978-1-4777-9084-7
1. History—Juvenile humor. I. Title.
PN6231.H47K56 2014
808.88'2—dc23
                        2013021314
Printed in the USA
SL003842US

CPSIA Compliance Information: Batch #BW14WM: For Further Information contact Windmill Books, New York, New York at 1-866-478-0556

CONTENTS

A mummy next to the Nile
Hadn't been out in a while,
So she strolled into town
In a long evening gown,
And everyone there
ran a mile.

Why did the Romans build straight roads?
So their soldiers didn't go around the bend.

What do the Greek gods drink with their breakfast?
Orange Zeus.

How was the Roman Empire cut in half?
With a pair of Caesars.

What do you get when you cross a mummy with a vampire bat?
A flying Band-Aid.

Why did the Roman colosseum have to close?
The lions had eaten up all the prophets!

What do you get in a five-star pyramid?
A tomb with a view.

Which Roman emperor is the windiest?
Au-gust-us.

What do you call armored pajamas?
Knight nighties.

What do you get if you cross a pharaoh with an auto mechanic?
A toot and car man.

Why was the Minotaur terrible at taking advice?
He was too bull-headed!

Why did the Egyptians make pyramids wide at the bottom and narrow at the top?
They were trying to make a point!

How did Noah see at night?
He used floodlights!

What can you say about the terrible mummy joke?
It sphinx.

Did you hear about the angry mummy?
He flipped his lid.

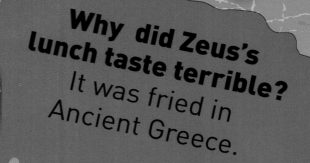

Why did Zeus's lunch taste terrible?
It was fried in Ancient Greece.

A Roman emperor asked his soothsayer to tell him the future. "I'm afraid your wife is going to die very suddenly," said the soothsayer. Two days later, the emperor's wife died. The emperor was very angry and ordered the soothsayer to come to him immediately. "Let's see if you can guess when *you* are going to die," said the emperor. Terrified, the soothsayer replied: "I don't know when I am going to die... but I do know that you will die two days later." The emperor left him alone!

How fast can a caveman run? It depends on the size of the dinosaur chasing him!

Why does it say "1286 BC" on the Ancient Egyptian's tomb? It's the registration of the chariot that ran him over!

Why do mummies make excellent spies? They're good at keeping things under wraps.

How do we know Moses wore a wig? Because sometimes he was seen with Aaron and sometimes without.

Why did Stone Age people eat sloths? Because they thought fast food was bad for you.

Why do mummies seldom take vacations? They don't want to relax and unwind.

How does the Roman cannibal feel about his mother-in-law? Gladiator.

What did the people of Minos pave their roads with? Mino-tar.

13

Why did Blackbeard wear headphones?
He liked listening to pirate radio.

What did the pirate say when his wooden leg got stuck in the freezer?
"Shiver me timbers!"

How did Columbus's men sleep on their ships?
With their eyes shut.

Why did the cowboy die with his boots on? Because he didn't want to stub his toes when he kicked the bucket.

Why was George Washington buried at Mount Vernon? Because he was dead.

What do you get when you cross a U.S. president with a shark? Jaws Washington.

Why did Christopher Columbus sail to America? Because it was too far to swim!

Who conquered half the world, laying eggs along the way?
Attila the Hen.

How much did the pirate pay for his peg leg and hook?
An arm and a leg.

What did the pirate cry as he fell overboard?
Water way to go!

Why do archers shoot arrows?
Could it be they are trying to get a point across?

An ancestor of mine came over on the Mayflower. Really? Which rat was he?

Abraham Lincoln's assassin had a table in a diner named after him. They called it the John Wilkes Booth.

A pirate with an eye patch, a hook, and a peg leg walks into a tavern. The bartender says, "You look like you've been in lots of sea battles. How did you get the peg leg?" The pirate answers, "Arr, a cannonball blew me leg right off!" "Wow!" says the bartender, "And how about the hook?" "Arr, me hand was eaten by a shark on the high seas!" "That's amazing! And the eye patch?" "Arr, a seagull pooped in me eye." Confused, the bartender asks, "How can you lose your eye from seagull poop?" "Well, it was me first day with the hook."

What is the moral of the story of Jonah and the whale?
You can't keep a good man down.

Which protest by a group of cats and dogs took place in 1773?
The Boston Flea Party.

Why don't pirates do the dishes before they walk the plank?
Because they wash up on shore later.

There was a bold
pirate of Boulder,
Whose cutlass was slung
from his shoulder.
He'd mighty fine notions
Of plundering oceans,
But his dad said: "Perhaps,
when you're older."

What did the executioner say to the prisoner?
Time to head off.

What do you get if a famous French general steps on a landmine?
Napoleon Blownapart.

How did the Hunchback of Notre Dame cure his sore throat?
He gargoyled.

A tired, hungry medieval peasant arrives at a roadside inn with a sign reading "George and the Dragon." He knocks on the door. The innkeeper's wife sticks her head out of the window. "Please can you spare some food?" the man asks. "No!" the woman shouts. "Could I have a drink of water?" "No!" she growls. "Could I at least use your bathroom?" "No!" she roars again. "Do you suppose," the man says, "I could speak to George?"

How do pirates make their money?
By hook or by crook.

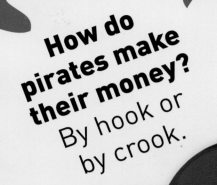

Why was the spearsman full of holes?
He kept getting the wrong end of the stick.

Visitor: Wow, you have a lot of flies buzzing around your horses. Do you ever shoo them?
Cowboy: No, we just let them go barefoot.

There was an old pirate named Jim
Who never learned how to swim
He fell off the deck
And broke his neck,
And that was the end of him.

Did you hear about the schoolgirl who was studying mythical monsters?
When her teacher asked her to name something half-man and half-beast, she said: "Buffalo Bill."

Who is the biggest gangster in the sea?
Al Caprawn.

Did prehistoric people hunt bear?
No, they wore clothes!

What do you call a highwayman with the flu?
Sick Turpin.

What do you call a pirate with four eyes?
A piiiirate.

What's yellow, tasty, and conquered most of Europe and Asia?
Genghis Khan on the cob.

What do you get if you cross a vampire with Al Capone?
A fangster.

Why did the witchfinder spend so long at the beach?
He was looking for a sandwich.

The executioner told his assistant to hold the basket in front of the chopping block.
"If we don't do this right," he said, "heads will roll."

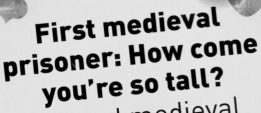

First medieval prisoner: How come you're so tall?
Second medieval prisoner: I was sentenced to a long stretch.

What happened when the gladiator put his head into a lion's mouth to count how many teeth the lion had? The lion closed its mouth to see how many heads the gladiator had!

After the great battle on the border between France and Germany, where did they bury the survivors? You don't bury survivors, silly!

If Friar Tuck was a monk, why did he get involved in a life of crime? It was his bad habit.

A three-legged dog walks into a saloon in the Old West. He hobbles up to the bar and says: "I'm looking for the man who shot my paw."

NUTTY KNIGHTS JOKES

Why do dragons breathe fire?
Because they don't like raw meat.

What happens when a queen burps?
She gets a royal pardon.

How was King Henry VIII different from normal husbands?
He married his wives first, and axed them afterward.

What did the ghost of Queen Bess say as it floated through the terrified woman's bedroom?
Don't worry, I'm just passing through.

What did the dragon say when he saw St. George in his shining armor?
Oh no, not more canned food!

Why didn't Henry VIII's marriages last?
At least two of his wives found him a pain in the neck.

Lady: We had boar for dinner last night.
Knight: Wild?
Lady: Let's just say he wasn't too happy.

Which British queen belched the most?
Queen Hic-toria.

It was once the custom for rich people to wear a fancy collar known as a ruff. The heir to the throne wore a small but fancy ruff, known as a dandy ruff. It was so tight that he fainted, and fell from the top of a tower. This proves that a little dandy ruff can cause the heir to fall out!

Which knight loved to throw unexpected parties?
Sir Prise!

What does an executioner read in the morning?
The noose-paper.

Why did the knight run around screaming for a can opener?
He had a bee in his suit of armor.

Why didn't Anne Boleyn stand still when she was being executed?
She wanted to run around the block.

The duke and the count had a fight.
The duke was out for the count.

Which knight did the dragon want to eat?
Sir Loin.

Which British queen was the fattest?
Mary, Queen of Scones.

Why did Henry VIII need an oxygen tank?
Because he couldn't breathe with no heir.

Where did Anastasia go?
I don't know. She must have been Romanov.

Why did the knight pull out of the archery contest?
He found it an arrowing experience.

Why do dragons sleep all day?
So they can fight knights.

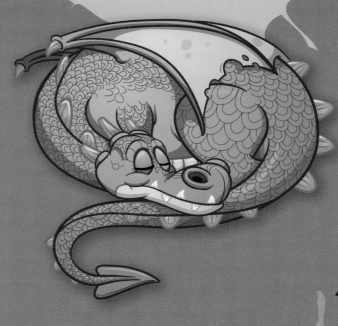

In days of old
When knights were bold,
Before toilets were invented,
They left their load
Along the road
And walked away contented.

How do you get ahead in life?
Become a royal executioner.

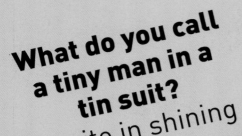

What do you call a tiny man in a tin suit?
A mite in shining armor.

Why did the knight always carry a bookmark?
He didn't want to lose his page!

Three knights came across a dragon in the forest. The dragon said, "I'm going to eat you." The first knight said, "Wait! Let's make a deal. Let each of us tell you something we think you can't do. If you can do it, you may eat us." The dragon agreed to the deal. Said the first knight: "Go to the barn and eat 16 rooms full of hay." The dragon did it. Said the second knight: "Drink half the water in the ocean." The dragon did this. The third knight burped and said: "Catch it and paint it green."

In days of old
When men were bold,
And pants were made of tin,
No mortal cry
Escaped a guy
Who sat down on a pin.

**Teacher:
If William
Braveheart
Wallace was alive
today, he would
be looked on as a
remarkable man.**
Pupil: Yes, he'd
be more than 600
years old!

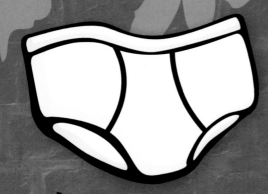

**Why did some
kings like
uprisings?**
They found them
a peasant
surprise.

**Why did the
queen have to
tell her eldest son
to stop being rude?**
She was having a
bad heir day!

Glossary

ancestor (AN-sess-tuhr) A relative who is a parent, a parent's parent, or a parent's parent's parent... and so on.

colosseum (KAH-luh-see-em) A Roman theatre.

cutlass (KUHT-luhss) A curved sword used by sailors.

Minotaur (MIH-no-tar) A mythological creature that is half man and half bull.

peat (PEET) A soil-like material made from plants that have rotted away.

soothsayer (SOOTH-say-ur) Someone who tells the future.

sphinx (SFINKS) A mythological creature with the body of a lion, the head of a woman.

Further Reading

Blank, Eva. *Jokelopedia*. New York, NY: Workman Publishing Company, 2006.

Connolly, Sean. *The Hysterical History Joke Book*. Laugh Out Loud. New York, NY: Windmill Books, 2013.

Hawkins, Jay. *Really Horrible History Facts*. Really Horrible Facts. New York, NY: Windmill Books, 2013.

Websites

For web resources related to the subject of this book, go to: www.windmillbooks.com/weblinks and select this book's title.

Index